THE SENSES

The Sense of Taste

by Mari Schuh

Consultant:
Eric H. Chudler, Ph.D.
Director, Neuroscience for Kids
University of Washington
Seattle, Wash.

BLASTOFF! READERS
4

BELLWETHER MEDIA · MINNEAPOLIS, MN

Note to Librarians, Teachers, and Parents:

Blastoff! Readers are carefully developed by literacy experts and combine standards-based content with developmentally-appropriate text.

Level 1 provides the most support through repetition of high-frequency words, light text, predictable sentence patterns, and strong visual support.

Level 2 offers early readers a bit more challenge through varied simple sentences, increased text load, and less repetition of high frequency words.

Level 3 advances early-fluent readers toward fluency through increased text and concept load, less reliance on visuals, longer sentences, and more literary language.

Level 4 builds reading stamina by providing more text per page, increased use of punctuation, greater variation in sentence patterns, and increasingly challenging vocabulary.

Level 5 encourages children to move from "learning to read" to "reading to learn" by providing even more text, varied writing styles, and less familiar topics.

Whichever book is right for your reader, Blastoff! Readers are the perfect books to build confidence and encourage a love of reading that will last a lifetime!

This edition first published in 2008 by Bellwether Media.

Library of Congress Cataloging-in-Publication Data
Schuh, Mari C, 1975–
 The sense of taste / by Mari Schuh.
   p. cm. — (Blastoff! readers. The senses)
Summary: "Introductory text explains the function and experience of the sense of taste. Intended for grades two through five"–Provided by publisher.
 Includes bibliographical references and index.
 ISBN-13: 978-1-60014-073-0 (hardcover : alk. paper)
 ISBN-10: 1-60014-073-4 (hardcover : alk. paper)
 1. Taste—Juvenile literature. I. Title.

 QP456.S38 2008
 612.8'6—dc22   2007015608

Contents

Your Sense of Taste

Your sense of taste allows you to enjoy food. Without your sense of taste, you wouldn't be able to taste salty popcorn or a sweet apple.

Your sense of taste tells you pickles can be sour. It tells you candy is sweet.

You use your tongue to taste. Your tongue has thousands of **taste buds**.

tongue

taste buds

They are found inside the bumps you can see on your tongue. Taste buds are too small to see.

Saliva in your mouth helps break down the food you eat. Chemicals in food soak into your taste buds.

Taste **sensors** are inside each taste bud. The sensors send messages to your brain about how the food tastes.

! fun fact

Girls often have more taste buds than boys.

Taste and Smell

Much of what you taste comes from your sense of smell. Your senses of taste and smell work together when you eat.

Your taste buds and your nose send messages to your brain. Then you know how food tastes. Have you ever pinched your nose when you had to take medicine? It doesn't taste as bad!

Kinds of Tastes

You have four main kinds of tastes. They are salty, sweet, sour, and bitter. Taste buds sense these four tastes. Some taste buds have sensors for more than one taste.

fun fact

You have almost 10,000 taste buds on your tongue.

What's your favorite fruit? Oranges and peaches have a sweet taste. Pretzels and chips have a salty taste.

Your parents' morning coffee tastes bitter. Lemons have a strong sour taste. That's why some people don't like to eat them.

Your tongue may even be able to sense a fifth taste. Scientists have discovered a taste they call **umami**. Umami isn't a strong taste. It mixes in with other tastes. You can taste umami in meats and cheeses.

fun fact

Some animals have more taste buds than people do. A pig's tongue has about 15,000 taste buds. A rabbit's tongue has about 17,000!

Animals and Taste

Some animals have a different sense of taste than people. Catfish can taste with their whole body!

Many insects have a great sense of taste. Flies, butterflies, and other insects taste with their feet! They walk on something to find out if it will taste good.

Your sense of taste helps keep you safe. Taste tells you about your food before you swallow it. You can use your sense of taste to find out if food is bad or too old to eat.

Your sense of taste helps you enjoy your food. How many kinds of foods have you tasted today? Were they sweet or salty? Were they sour or bitter?

Glossary

saliva—a liquid inside your mouth; saliva helps break down your food so you can taste it.

sensor—the parts of your body that send messages to your nerves and brain

taste buds—very small parts of your tongue that sense tastes

umami—a fifth taste; the umami taste is found in meat and cheese.

To Learn More

AT THE LIBRARY
Barraclough, Sue. *What Can I Taste?* Chicago, Ill.: Raintree, 2005.

Mackill, Mary. *Tasting*. Chicago, Ill.: Heinmann, 2006.

Pryor, Kimberley Jane. *Tasting*. Philadelphia, Pa.: Chelsea Clubhouse, 2004.

ON THE WEB
Learning more about taste is as easy as 1, 2, 3.

1. Go to www.factsurfer.com

2. Enter "taste" into search box.

3. Click the "Surf" button and you will see a list of related web sites.

With factsurfer.com, finding more information is just a click away.

Index